T0149417

For the LOVE of SELF

The Proven Tools and Strategies
for Healing My Life

Kaylene Hay

BALBOA.
PRESS

A DIVISION OF HAY HOUSE

Balboa Press books may be ordered through booksellers or by contacting:

Balboa Press
A Division of Hay House
1663 Liberty Drive
Bloomington, IN 47403
www.balboapress.com.au
1 (877) 407-4847

Cover Graphics/Art Credit - Leonie Bartlett

Print information available on the last page.

ISBN: 978-1-5043-1458-9 (sc)
ISBN: 978-1-5043-1459-6 (e)

Balboa Press rev. date: 09/07/2018

The past is what influenced my life's choices,
Now my new beliefs continue to create a better future.

CONTENTS

FOREWORD

Kaylene Hay is a strong and independent woman, displaying a caring and compassionate approach as an intuitive healer. Through dedication, extensive study and research, she has healed many of her life challenges. Kaylene has also counselled many people to acknowledge, address, and overcome their own illnesses and life patterns.

If you have picked up this book, congratulations! It means you are searching for answers to whatever is troubling you right now. Read on as the answer to your dilemma could just be in the following pages.

Kaylene, thank you for your courage in writing this book about your own life story, and bless you, to all who read it.

Love to you all.

Linda Christa~Clay
Messenger of the Angels & Spiritual Clairvoyant Healer

INTRODUCTION

In this "self-help" book, you will find the tools and strategies that assisted me achieve the healing outcomes I desired without the use of surgery or drugs. This could also be the right way for you.

♥ I believe that, with the help of my Angels, guides, and spirit family, I chose the perfect set of circumstances for my soul's growth before coming into this life.

The many challenges that came my way were all my soul's pre-life choices. My parents were not responsible in any way. They actually had created the perfect environment for me to learn my lessons, and grow stronger physically, mentally, emotionally, and spiritually. Everything is always as it's meant to be even if it doesn't appear to be that way at the time. Learning to trust the process of life can be a bit confusing, but once there is understanding, great progress can be made.

♥ I believe that loving ourselves is the first major step to implementing any changes that we need to make in our life.

There is no point comparing yourself to another or trying to compete for something that isn't right for you. Just be your authentic self and live the life you were born for. Set out to find what your passion is and follow it to create the life that you've always wanted.

♥ I believe that dis-ease, even cancer, can be created by repetitive thoughts and emotions like guilt, hurt, resentment, anger, shame, and unworthiness. But you can change and heal anything if you're willing to do the inner work.

Change is the only consistent thing in life, so rather than running away from trying circumstances, just say, "Bring it on!" as it must be happening for a reason. To heal the complex and sometimes confusing situations, it's necessary to work through them in a positive, step by step way. This helps discover what really is happening so that any negative beliefs can be addressed and rectified. The rewards, such as feeling as if a burden has been lifted from your shoulders, proves that all the effort is certainly worth it.

♥ I believe the help I need to heal any challenge is always available to me if I ask the questions. The answers are within.

We are all here to learn and grow from our life's experience. One way is no better than another. It's your choice of how you will overcome/heal the issues behind any challenges you are presented with. The proven tools and strategies that worked for me could work for you as well. Our lives are a work-in-progress and there will always be something to understand, accept, and let go of, until it's our time to go home/heaven.

♥ I believe that we are never given any more than we can handle.

It may seem a little simplistic but the truth is, we never know our inner strength, courage, and faith, until we are faced with something that seems insurmountable at the time. This builds the trust in ourselves to face any adversity with more calmness and determination than we thought was possible. We are powerful beings.

♥ I believe that ultimately it's up to each individual to take responsibility for their own actions, health, and well-being.

For everything we do in life, there is a cause and an effect. If you eat too much lets say, you are most likely to put on weight even though that is not what you wanted. Balance is the key to life no matter what you're doing. Find the right balance in all areas of your life, and life will work much more harmoniously for you.

♥ I believe that the right people and information will come into our life for the lessons, growth, and healing, that we need.

When introduced to Louise L. Hay's philosophies, what Louise had to say just made good sense to me. It's obvious now that her work was going to be very important in healing my sexual abuse, and the issues that were generated from that. But of course I didn't know that then.

PRELUDE AND TIMELINE

Some important milestones in my life:

- ♥ Born Kaylene Anne (nickname Lucy) Bland in Kingaroy, Queensland, Australia on 28.4.1950. These numbers add up to 11, which is my personal birth number. It's also a Master Number.
- ♥ Right eye turned in (squint) at four months
- ♥ Moved fifteen times up until I was eighteen (refer to "The Bland Family's Journey")
- ♥ Wore a patch over right eye then got glasses at age four
- ♥ 1955 – 1958 Our family of eight lived in a small hut at Sterlings Crossing Forestry Camp
- ♥ 1956 Started school at Imbil
- ♥ 1966, at sixteen, left home and went to work at the Court House in Gympie. It was a well-paid Government position.
- ♥ 1969, at nineteen, fiancé jilted me three weeks prior to wedding
- ♥ 1970 met Bill 6.6.1970. These numbers add up to 11 as well, my personal birth number. (I feel it was a date with destiny and I followed him to Port Moresby. Not as exciting as it may sound, but certainly worth the effort.)
- ♥ 1971 Married Bill in Port Moresby on 2nd July
- ♥ 1972 Leanne was born in Port Moresby on 22nd January
- ♥ 1974 Moved to Bundaberg to start own taxation and accountancy business
- ♥ 1974 Karen was born on 21st December
- ♥ 1976 First eye surgery
- ♥ 1976 Built our home in Avoca, Bundaberg (owner/builder)

- 1977 Susan was born on 26th August
- 1978 Second eye surgery
- 1987 Started wearing two hearing aids
- 1988 Joined the Inner Peace Movement. Started learning about the power of the mind, positive thinking, past lives, and the Laws of the Universe. Interesting times.
- 1990 and onwards, was introduced to Reiki, Louise L. Hay's philosophies in *You Can Heal Your Life*, and many other healing modalities, including crystals
- 1993 Attuned to Reiki First Degree
- 1997 Attuned to Reiki Second Degree
- 1999 Undertook teacher training in Louise Hay's work and started teaching workshops and study courses
- 2001 Easter - Bill and I separated
- 2001 May - Diagnosed with vaginal cancer
- 2001 Attuned to Reiki *Jin Kei Do* Master Level on 19.9.2001. These numbers add up to 22, meaning "Self-mastery", and another Master Number. I commenced teaching and attuning students soon after.
- 2002 Moved to Brisbane
- 2002 Bill and I reunited on 5th October
- 2002 Qualified as an Angel Intuitive Practitioner with Doreen Virtue PhD.
- 2004 Started writing this book but shelved it as uncertain what to do.
- 2005 Studied floristry and worked in the industry for some time
- 2015 Attuned to *Rahanni* (meaning 'Of One Heart') *Celestial Healing*
- 2016 Prompted to continue writing my book (While discussing my book with Bill on our way into the city, I saw a large white billboard. The message on it, in purple writing said, "Your Story Changes Lives".) Now that's the type of sign that couldn't be ignored. So I started attending biography classes to help me with this creative project.

THE BLAND FAMILY'S JOURNEY

1946, June	Dad (Keneth Stanley Bland) arrived back from serving in the second World War
1946, June	Dad and Mum (Coreen Mildred Stutz) got married
1946, July	Stutz farm, Teddington, Maryborough
1946, September	Moved to Maryborough
1947, February	Moved to Teddington Road (Carol Lyn born 26.3.1947)
1947, July	Moved to Maryborough
1948, May	Moved to another place in Maryborough
1948, September	Dad worked in Kingaroy and came back to Maryborough on weekends
1948, November	Moved to Hervey Bay (Lynette Kay born 11.11.1948)
1948, November	Moved to Kingaroy (three weeks only)
1948, December	Moved again in Kingaroy
1949, August	Moved to Kumbia
1949, November	Moved to Alice Creek (Kaylene Anne (Lucy) born 28.4.1950)
1951, April	Moved to Tingoora (Janet Maree born 12.5.1951)
1951, August	Moved to Tinana
1952, February	Moved to Mondure and Tingoora
1952, April	Moved to Wondai (Kenneth Norman John born 1.12.1953)
1954, May	Moved to Calico Creek

1955, September	Moved to shed at Calico Creek (ten days)
1955, September	Moved to Sterlings Crossing Camp. (Wendy Gail born 29.1.1957)
1959, April	Moved into a house at Sterlings Crossing, near Imbil
1960, April	Moved to Cedar Pocket, near Gympie
1962, April	Moved to Ross Creek
1962, August	Ross Creek school closed. Transferred to Cootharaba Road School.
1962, October	Moved to Goomboorian, outside Gympie
1963, May	Moved to Kia Ora, outside Gympie
1967, October	Moved to Gympie
1968, January	Moved again in Gympie
1971, January	Moved to Rockhampton
1971, April	I left home and went to live with Bill in Port Moresby.

Chapter 1

THE IMPACT OF STERLINGS CROSSING

From 1955 to 1958, our family of eight (referred to as the Bland Tribe by many), lived in a small hut at the Sterlings Crossing Forestry Camp, which is about thirty-four kilometres west of Gympie, Queesland. The hut consisted of half-timber walls, and the rest was canvas. My Dad learnt carpentry when he was released from the army, so he was able to build another room on the side to accommodate us all. We previously lived on a farm at Calico Creek. That ended badly, but the upside was Dad getting a full-time job grafting pine trees in the Imbil Forestry, seven kilometres from where we lived. To earn extra money, he also picked pineapples on a farm when he could.

It was whooping cough season during this time. From memory, at least three of the children contracted it. So you can imagine the household was under a lot of pressure, and my Mum really didn't cope well, particularly with Dad working away every day. The amount of stress certainly contributed to her debilitating migraines.

It's interesting to note that although I missed out on having whooping cough then, I managed to have my turn in 2010 and a second, lesser case in 2011. Not very pleasant as an adult.

There was a lovely little creek at Sterlings Crossing where everyone went for a swim. My fear of water began then. At about six years old, my Dad left me in the middle of this creek, where my feet couldn't touch the bottom, and said, "Swim!" Now that may work for some, but it certainly didn't work for me. My fear was enormous.

I do remember fondly that there were many bottle brush trees lining this creek, and I fell in love with their soft, red-bristled flowers. Now, we live next to a nature reserve, so I've planted some miniature bottle brush trees to attract the birds.

Our home wasn't a palace to be sure. There was the outside shower, cold of course, so warm baths for the smaller children were in the outside concrete wash-tubs, and there was also the "thunderbox" dunny down the back yard. Both were often infested with red back spiders, which Dad used to kill or chase away by using burning newspaper. So you can imagine any trip to the shower or toilet was very short. To this day I still go cold all over when I see a red back spider, whether real or in a picture, although I think they are very beautiful.

A HUT at Sterlings Crossing forestry camp.
we lived in one from before Xmas (1955 until moving into a house June 1958

We had no electricity, so kerosene lanterns provided the lighting, which meant early nights for all. The cooking took place on a wood stove that also provided any heating. Most hot water, which was used for the adults' baths, was generated by the outside copper boiler. This was also used to do all the washing, which was hung on rope lines strung between two posts. Just think about the changing/washing of sheets on all our beds and the towels everyone used as well as all the clothing. Mind-boggling!

We eventually had a chook run that provided eggs and a tasty roast chicken dinner from time to time, and we used to make butter from the milk of our resident cow. Dad milked her twice a day. And, of course, vege gardens were all "the rage", or may I say "survival", in those days. There was always plenty to do, and each of us had assigned duties before and after school.

My schooling started in 1956 with a seven kilometre bus ride to and from Imbil State School. This is when the bullying started and continued until I decided to take this matter into my own hands, literally. But this occurred when I was older, as you will read later.

For me, one of the highlights of living at Sterlings Crossing was going out very early in the morning, while there was still dew on the grass, and being with nature. Sometimes I was lucky enough to catch a frilly lizard and take it home with me to feed it flies while it lazed on our canna plants. Not to mention, fishing in the local stream. As a young child, these activities were just great and transported me away from all the "not so pleasant" happenings in my life.

Some twenty years ago, in the late 1990's, my good friend Linda Christa~Clay and I made a nostalgic journey back to Sterlings Crossing, Imbil, and around the Forestry. The most noticeable thing was that all the huts were gone, so it was hard to imagine my life there. I also realised my perception of distances, and so on, seemed different now, not to say it wasn't real for me at the time.

Chapter 2

A PIVOTAL MOMENT IN TIME

It was so amazing! I looked in the mirror, and my right eye was straight for the first time in over twenty-five years. A faint stirring of excitement and confidence seeped into my being that contributed to some very welcome changes in my life. This was 1976.

I was born in 1950, the third child of six, five girls and one boy. At about four months of age, my right eye turned in quite badly. Mum thought it might have resulted from me falling off the bed. My parents sought help with it. In those days, a patch was used to cover each eye, alternating daily, to hopefully strengthen the weak one. It didn't seem to work. It just made me very frustrated and difficult to get along with.

At about age four, I got my first pair of glasses, which didn't really help either. They just cost Mum and Dad lots of money with breakages and me losing them. But I continued to wear them because they were supposed to help strengthen and possibly straighten my eye. My specialist wouldn't do an operation on "the squint". He felt the chances of my eye turning outward were too great, and that would look worse than being turned in. Family members referred to me as "You Poor Little Thing", so I grew up with a victim mentality. I felt very unlovable and unworthy.

We moved fifteen times up until I was eighteen (refer to The Bland Family's Journey). I found it hard to make friends as it seemed I was always the "new kid on the block" and that attracted sometimes-unwanted attention. My sister Janet was my best friend, and we did most things together until we both got married. Moving all the time wasn't enjoyable for me, but others may have seen it as an exciting adventure.

In my childhood, times were tough in many ways. My parents found it hard to cope with their life's challenges. Dad was a very hard worker but quite an angry man. He belittled my mother, calling her names, yelling, and sometimes getting physical. So there was lots of crying followed by silence, and then everything seemed to be OK again. Until the next time. This took its' toll on me, and I became very fearful. Somehow it seemed my responsibility to try "to fix" the problem. But, of course, that wasn't possible. My life seemed like a rollercoaster ride, and it felt like I was walking on eggshells a lot, never knowing what mood would be in the house at any time.

During my school years, my self-esteem was pretty low because of the bullying and name-calling by children who found it entertaining and fun. About the age of twelve, a boy from a nearby farm continually called me "four eyes" and made fun of me. One day I finally had enough. Pushing him to the ground and sitting on his belly, I gave him a pounding he would always remember. After that, he never called me names again. It may not have been the right way to handle the situation, but it sure felt empowering! The boy's father even went to talk to my Dad about the events, but Dad didn't punish me for it. He may have been just a little proud of me for standing up for myself.

Many years later we saw each other at a function. Even though I remembered his name, neither of us seemed to have a need to say hi and have a trip down memory lane.

Developing some extrovert behaviours, and never looking straight at anyone, became my way to cover for my insecurities as my turned eye was very off-putting. No one knew where to look at me.

I got married in Port Moresby in 1971. We worked there for three years before Bill and I moved back to Bundaberg in 1974, where we started our taxation and accountancy practice.

A newly qualified eye specialist came to town and happened to move into an office next to our business. Very convenient. At my usual check-up, he asked me if I had considered having surgery for my right eye "squint". When I told him my original specialist wouldn't do it, he said he would be happy to give it a shot, but he still only gave me a fifty/fifty chance of improvement. That was enough for me. I was in and prepared to take the chance.

Hope and happiness filled me when I awoke from the surgery to see that my eye was straight. Looking directly at people was normal now, and there was no reason to be embarrassed anymore. My eye specialist suggested contact lenses were even a possibility.

Unfortunately, over the next year, my eye started to turn back, and contact lenses would have only accentuated the turn in my eye. So a second surgery was performed. The muscle was tightened from my good eye, which could help keep my right eye straighter. This helped, and to this day, my eye is much improved and looks straight most of the time. However, there was no change in the percentage of sight in that eye. But as they say, "You don't miss what you've never had." I have made necessary adjustments throughout my life to accommodate this, and I am always grateful for the ten percent long-range vision that I do have.

Since reading and exploring healing, metaphysics (looking into the mental and emotional causes of issues), and understanding the laws of the Universe, I realized that it wasn't the fall off the bed that caused my eye to turn. That was only one part of it. Seeing how my Mum and Dad interacted with each other had a huge effect on me mentally and emotionally. This gave me a distorted view of how relationships work. How could two people who loved each other act the way they did towards each other. Impressions of what "love" meant were very confusing to me.

Below is an explanation from the material I have read:-

Being the right eye - my physical side.

Long sightedness - there is a fear of the present.

The affirmation used to help heal and reverse this fear was "I am safe in this moment. I see that clearly".

But at the end of the day, seeing my eye straight now is the focus as the whole situation has been forgiven and healed.

With the knowledge and awareness gained through reading "self-help" books, I believe that my Mum and Dad were doing the best they knew how under the circumstances. This helped me forgive them and heal my negative beliefs about it all. It is understood now that my Dad was most likely suffering from "Post Traumatic Stress Disorder" as a result of serving as a field ambulance officer in the second World War. On returning home, there was no medical treatment available to help him, or others, come to terms with what happened in the war. These days, I just feel great compassion for what he had endured.

Chapter 3

PRECIOUS WATER

Water is a precious commodity, but is even more so when living on a farm, there's crops to grow and cattle to sustain so every drop is important. We milked about seventy head of cows all year round.

Now as an eleven year old, I learnt a very dear lesson. My younger sister Janet and I were in charge of cleaning up the cow bales after the morning milking. There was the separator to clean and the floors needed to be washed. It was important that all utensils would be ready for the afternoon milking.

Dad had only re-cemented the handle on our water tank at the cow bales the day before. The concrete was still not set properly. Of course we didn't really know that, we were just kids. Our help was very much needed and at times I felt we were given too much responsibility.

The time came to get water for the washing up. We were unsure if it was safe to turn the handle. Janet said it should be OK to do it, so I did. Can you imagine our disbelief when the whole handle and concrete came away from the tank. All the precious water was just pouring out. We got a milk can and frantically saved what we could. Sadly only one milk can was filled. I felt sick but accepted the responsibility for what happened because I was the one who had pulled the handle.

Panic set in and we didn't know what to do. Mum was so upset because she didn't know what Dad would do when he realised what we had done. We were terrified and hid behind the door in our bedroom, holding our breath waiting for him to come home. When Dad came home, he was so devastated by the loss of water that he didn't do anything to us. The belting we anticipated never happened. He did say that we would have to carry water from the dam as there was a bad drought at the time, but he never enforced this. To this day, I still get upset when I see water being wasted.

Our worst fear wasn't realised after all. So much energy was wasted worrying about what my Dad would say and do. Fear is a crippling emotion. Understandable though.

But there is an even more important lesson here I feel and that is, don't do something if you're not sure that it is the right thing to do. Learn to trust and follow your own gut instincts/intuition and not do what someone else says.

Chapter 4

QUITTING THE CIGARETTE HABIT

This particular Tuesday in July, 1993 was going to be different from every other Tuesday because I didn't go for the first cigarette of the day. Could this be the day?

As a young teenager growing up on a farm at Kia Ora which is twenty-six kilometres outside of Gympie, Queensland, I started smoking cigarettes. My eldest sister taught me how to do the "draw back", but to be fair, I did ask her to show me. Peter Styvesant was my favourite, although menthol ones were enjoyed as well. It seemed to be the "in" thing to do and I would do anything to fit in with the crowd. Picking beans and peas at nearby farms on weekends was my way of earning money. The pay was three pence a pound of produce (this was before decimal currency came in on 14.2.1966 - maybe two cents per 500 grams today - which was normal in those days). This is how the cigarettes were paid for. Dad would confiscate any cigarettes he found, even though they were cleverly hidden. It seems parents know more than we give them credit for. Leaving home at sixteen and going to work in Gympie, Dad couldn't stop me then from buying and smoking cigarettes.

It seemed everyone used to smoke in those days and we could smoke anywhere. There were no restrictions really. Thinking about it now, I cringe as there had been no thought for any non-smoker who was around me. It was very selfish and inconsiderate of me.

Some forty-five years ago when having a check-up for my first pregnancy, my doctor never asked me if I was a smoker. It was something that wasn't even discussed back then. Smoking was a part of my life and I continued this habit during all of my three pregnancies. Even cutting back on the cigarettes during these times, I was oblivious to the damage that could have been caused.

Over the years cigarettes had become my crutch. They were my best friend when coping with stressful and challenging life situations. Reaching for a cigarette fix at those times was normal as I felt I couldn't cope without them. The temporary relief was very much enjoyed.

Some family members pressured me regularly to give up cigarettes but the timing/my timing had to be right, mentally and emotionally. There's a great saying, "When you know better, you do better". Forgiving myself for my ignorance and selfish attitude was a start, but it couldn't change what had already happened.

After being attuned to Reiki (Universal life force energy – refer to Chapter 5 for more information) in February 1993, the decision was made to give up my thirty year addiction to twenty plus cigarettes a day. My focus now was conducting healing treatments on others. The smell of cigarettes on my breath, hands, and clothes wouldn't have been pleasant for my clients. This became my incentive to get serious about ditching the cigarettes once and for all.

At this time, Louise L. Hay's philosophies in *You Can Heal Your Life* had been introduced to me and her theories sounded exciting and workable. This helped me change my negative thoughts and behaviours to a new way of positive thinking. Here were two powerful tools at my disposal. Little did I know just what would be revealed as I started to look into why certain things were happening in my life.

The following affirmation was made up to use, "I lovingly and willingly release the need for nicotine", as nicotine is what we get addicted to. Studies have proven that nicotine is in the same category as heroin addiction. Well this affirmation was said in my mind and out loud every day, many times, but still smoking of course. Using Reiki healing on myself whenever possible helped the process as well. Finally after five months of continually saying the affirmation, I just stopped. Yes, it was that Tuesday morning back in July when I didn't light up that first cigarette of the day like I normally would.

And the good news is - that was it! No cigarette has passed my lips since then. Even better, the craving for one stopped as well. So the theory of continually using an affirmation to change a situation had been proven to me. Louise Hay's philosophy worked, and I felt very empowered. A great example of the power of the mind.

Chapter 5

REIKI JIN KEI DO
(The Way of Compassion and Wisdom)

After attending an information evening conducted by Reiki Master, Faye Wenke, in 1993, I decided to join her weekend workshop and she attuned me to First Degree. Reiki Masters have the ability, through years of training, to attune other people to this universal energy. My interest was instant and I thought it was magic when I started using it on myself and others and saw the results that were achieved. I continued my training and was attuned to Reiki Second Degree in 1997 and eventually on to completing my Masters training in September 2001. The benefits were so natural and wonderful that I conducted workshops myself and attuned students so they could learn to use it for their own self-healing as well.

The following information has been gathered from attending many workshops over the years.

The Spiritual Principles of Reiki Jin Kei Do

Be mindful each moment of your day

~ to observe the arising of greed, anger and delusion, looking deeper for their true cause,

~ to appreciate the gift of life and be compassionate to all beings,

~ to find the right livelihood and be honest in your work,

~ to see within, the ever changing nature of your mind and body,

~ to merge with the universal nature of the mind as Reiki flows within you.

By following these ideals daily, your mind and body will transform and deep healing will follow.

Reiki (pronounced ray-key) is a Japanese word representing the underlying force behind every living being. It is this essential energy that supports all life, therefore, in the broadest translation of the word, Reiki means life itself.

Reiki is an ancient healing form which was rediscovered in the late 1800's by a Japanese scholar, Dr Mikao Usui, after undertaking an extensive study of the healing phenomenon of history's greatest spiritual leaders. He dedicated the rest of his life to the practice and teaching of this method he named Reiki.

Reiki *Jin Kei Do* follows the Eastern lineage of Masters, traditionally Buddhist healing monks, who were empowered by Dr Usui with Reiki.

Reiki is not a belief system or religion and is a non-invasive, gentle, yet powerful method of healing. It complements any type of healing whether it be orthodox, as in Western medicine, or natural therapies such as herbal medicine, homeopathy, or nutritional therapy. It can be practised by anyone once you have been attuned to this energy by a Master, who has undertaken the necessary training to do so. Once you have been attuned, you have access to this universal healing energy forever.

Reiki refers to a method of healing in which this energy is accessed at a deep level and is absorbed by every cell in the body. When this energy is flowing in a balanced way, the mind and body become relaxed, allowing the organs and body systems to begin to function better. This accelerates the body's healing ability and opens the mind to the underlying causes of dis-ease and pain, thus providing support and balance in our life, not only at a physical level, but emotionally, mentally and spiritually as well. It is also very effective on animals and plants.

Reiki Healing Session

Reiki *Jin Kei Do* healing is performed on and off your body (fully clothed) in a seated position or lying on a therapy table, working in the auric field to intensify the energy. The practitioner simply places his/her hands in various positions around your head and body allowing the energy to flow through him/her to you. This promotes deep relaxation and a feeling of peace and well-being. The healing session usually lasts around an hour. What is so wonderful about giving a healing to another person is that the healer gets the benefit as well, it's reciprocal.

Distant healing sessions can also be conducted using Reiki symbols to connect with you. These are taught in Reiki classes. The effects of the healing and overall outcome are the same as if you were having a healing in person.

Some benefits of Reiki achieved for myself:

- ♥ Self-healing is the main basis for Reiki
- ♥ It goes to the root cause of any issue so this helps identify what needs attention.
- ♥ Able to give myself healing whenever I need it for anything, and to help with any situation as the energy can be accessed at any time.
- ♥ Assisted me in quitting the cigarette habit
- ♥ Calms me down

Eg. Waking up in the middle of the night, heart pounding and thinking about a difficult situation, but by giving myself some Reiki healing, it helps me to switch off the fear. This calms me down which allows me to go back to sleep.

♥ Helped me heal from emotional, mental and physical traumas
♥ It's given me the ability to send healing to people, places, and world events that need it.
♥ And so much more …

General benefits of Reiki for others:

♥ Releases stress and promotes deep relaxation
♥ Eases pain
♥ Relieves colds, flu, headaches, burns, cuts, nausea, allergies, and sports injuries etc.
♥ Aids in the withdrawal of addictive drugs
♥ Improves memory, creativity and learning ability
♥ Accelerates healing on all levels
♥ Helps increase confidence and self esteem

Testimonials from some of my clients

1. Kaylene's healing hands did wonders to my body after a major operation. After every treatment my whole body felt wonderfully relaxed without any pain. I believe Kaylene has been given a special healing power to help many others. (Posted by Kaye)

2. Over the past 3 years, I have had the opportunity to receive many Reiki treatments and I found that Kaylene carried out her treatments in a professional manner but always with a kindness and a gentleness befitting her gift as a healer. (Posted by Caroline)

3. Kaylene performed distance healing on my mouth cyst. I was told by doctors that it would have to be surgically removed. After having a consultation with a plastic surgeon I did not wish to go down that path due to many complications. The cyst had already been present for around 8 weeks. I approached Kaylene and in a short space of time the cyst had started to disappear. This was a fantastic result for both of us. Thank you Kaylene. (Posted by Steven)

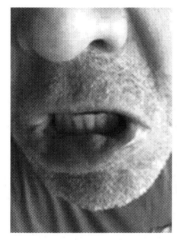 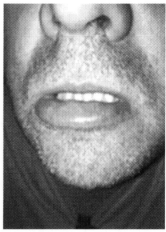

PS: Apart from the initial sighting of the cyst, the only contact with my client was by way of "distant" healing from my healing room at home. Steven lives about twelve kilometres away. I had also given him a relevant affirmation to say during the healing process which I feel helped with the overall positive outcome.

From the first healing connection with Steven, it took about four weeks of sending regular healing to the cyst for it to be dissolved and healed.

So it's just another example to show that we are all connected. Healing takes place with a therapist in person, or can be sent to a person, or situation, with the use of special symbols. The result will still be the same.

There is no guarantee though of what benefits will be gained in a Reiki healing session as the recipient can only receive whatever is for their highest good at that time.

Chapter 6

THE POWER OF PRAYER

Many years ago around the late 1990's, my husband Bill attended a seminar on Fraser Island, Queensland (the largest sand island in the world). We stayed at the Kingfisher Bay Resort overlooking Sandy Straight. It was a magical place.

While he was at the seminar, a long leisurely walk through the tropical rain forest seemed the perfect activity to fill in my time. The beauty and tranquility really beckoned me to explore and savour nature at its' best. Enjoying the experience so much, I took off my glasses, and also took out my two hearing aids, so that this beautiful environment could be perceived through all my senses naturally. These were all placed in the pocket of my shirt and then continued on my way.

Wanting to take a closer look at a flower, my glasses were needed to appreciate its' unique and intricate make-up. Leaving my glasses on after that, I continued walking. It was time to turn around and go back to our accommodation as Bill's seminar would be finished and we had agreed to meet for lunch. Reaching into my pocket to get my hearing aids out, you can imagine my horror when realising my pocket was empty (the hearing aids must've fallen out while getting my glasses). Now as my hearing loss is quite severe, I am unable to function very well without them. The $4000 it would cost to replace them was making me panic because of our financial situation at the time.

Hopefully retracing my original steps through the sand, and with my heart pounding, I sat down on a seat. I closed my eyes and started praying silently, "Please Angels, help me find my hearing aids as I really need them". And "Nothing is lost in the eyes of God". As my aids were "flesh coloured", they would be camouflaged very well in the sand. After a while, some people walked past which broke my reverie. Getting up I kept walking, when all of a sudden I just stopped and felt compelled to look down, and there they were, my two hearing aids lying side by side in the sand. Can you believe that? Anyone could've walked on them, but fortunately they were unharmed, and I was very relieved to have them back. I truly believe that God, and the Angels, were with me that day, heard my prayers, and helped me find my hearing aids. Very grateful.

They are looked after much better these days. If they are not in my ears, they are in their case and have never been lost again.

Chapter 7

LETTING GO OF FEARS

Back in 1997 when I was forty-seven and very committed to my personal/spiritual growth, an invitation arrived in the post to attend a week long workshop. It was structured around fears, how to work through them, and let them go. Well, there was an instant knowing that it would be a good idea to join this workshop. My life revolved around many fears and it was time that some of them were dealt with. This was an opportunity not to be missed.

A medical examination and a stress test were required by a Doctor to check my suitability for the course. There wasn't any other information available about what was involved, just where and when to meet and all would be explained then. This should have set off alarm bells, but it would seem I wasn't hearing them.

There were seventy participants who joined that night and we were put into seven groups of ten. Each person within the group was designated a partner, mine was Mark – yes a male. Once we signed our Confidentiality/Personal Responsibility Agreement, we were only given instructions which were needed at that time. We were then guided to get on a bus. Now this bus had blackened windows so we had no idea where we were going.

The theory seemed to be, let's get into fears straight away. You can imagine most of us were anxious before we even went anywhere.

We drove all night and I still don't know to this day where we went. When we arrived at our destination, tent equipment was handed out for us to assemble. Now I might be strong and can do many things, putting up a tent wasn't one of them. It seems that Mark had no skills in this area either. Great start. We eventually managed to get the tent up somehow and it was time for more instructions.

The first morning, and every other morning, we had to be up at day break and go for a nude swim in the creek. Oh no, I had to take my clothes off in front of everybody. Then my glasses and hearing aids were removed as well. I truly felt naked, vulnerable, and scared. To me it was my worst nightmare. And to top that off, one of my greatest fears was, you guessed it – *water* – or being in water (refer to the story in Chapter 1, "The Impact of Sterlings Crossing"). Luckily there were others who felt the same way, so knowing this fact was a little comforting.

Many activities were undertaken that week, climbing tight ropes, abseiling, orienteering, rock climbing and so on. I felt really useless and out of my depth as I hadn't attempted any of these things before. You can imagine the heart palpitations, the dry mouth, and the stomach screwed up in knots as each activity was explained and what was expected, let alone actually doing them.

Towards the end of the week, this particular day was very important. We had to write all of our fears down on a piece of paper and keep it with us during the day.

Some of the organisers of this workshop were building a big fire, a bit like what the American Indians would build. It was tended all day. Later that evening, we all held hands and chanted as we walked slowly around and around the fire for a very long time. Then one by one we were told to throw our paper, with all the fears written on it, into the fire. Can you imagine my utter disbelief when my piece of paper didn't make it into the fire. After all the work we had done during the week, here I was still afraid to let go of my fears. Just mortified. The leader of the group picked up my piece of paper and put it in the fire for me. She explained that it may not have any impact on letting go of my fears after all. It's definitely not the same as doing it for myself. My disappointment was very overwhelming.

By now we were tired and needing our bed but there was something more we still had to do that night. Really?

Most of the wood in the fire had burned down to coals by then. The men who had been tending the fire started to rake the coals into a rectangle shape about one metre wide and three metres long. Then one by one we were invited to walk across the coals. Traditional fire walking, think about it. What an experience! It was easy and I didn't sustain any burns. My belief was strong by continually affirming that this could be achieved. Then we went through the coals again, two at a time, to see if our partner was harbouring any fear of being burnt. No one had their feet burnt that night. Everything else we had achieved during that week seemed insignificant compared to the experience of the "Fire Walk".

To this day, my memory of that fire walk is still very vivid, always reminding me just how powerful my mind can be with focus and intent. Lesson well learnt.

Chapter 8

ARCHANGEL MICHAEL TO THE RESCUE

While Bill and I were travelling on a group bus tour through Europe, we were always told to lock our personal papers away when we left our hotel. This day we had already left when we realised that our Passports hadn't been locked away into the suitcase. As there was no time to go back, there was only one thing that could be done. I called on the Angels to protect our "stuff" until we got back. I was very surprised and excited when in my mind's eye, a big, burly, and tall Archangel Michael (who is the Angel of Protection) turned up. His arms were folded across his chest, feet astride, and with the energy that said, "No one, but no one, will be getting past me into this room." Chuckling to myself, I said a very big thank you to him for being of service to us. Our belongings were kept safe of course until we returned. Whenever going out now, this vision is used knowing that Archangel Michael will be there to protect my home.

It has been recorded in many books that the Universe has seven main Archangels and they are listed below including their attributes:-

Archangel Michael is for courage, strength, truth, integrity, and protection. He will protect you on journeys, your home, and your car. He protects you physically, mentally, and emotionally.

Archangel Raphael is for healing, wholeness, and unity. If you need healing in any way he will heal your mind, body, and soul. He can also get your life back on track again.

Archangel Chamuel is for unconditional love, relationships, and nurturing. If you are feeling depressed or in despair, he will surround you with healing love.

Archangel Gabriel is for guidance, vision, and inspiration. He will help you on your path, no matter what. He will guide you when moving house, changing career, or starting a family.

Archangel Jophiel is for spiritual knowledge and wisdom, illumination, and joy. He will awaken you to your spiritual path. If you need inspiration when writing, call him.

Archangel Uriel is for peace and tranquillity. He will help calm tension in your solar plexus and help you to find inner peace.

Archangel Zadkiel is for forgiveness, mercy, and tolerance. He will purify your mind, body, and soul from negative thoughts.

As you can see, Archangel Michael has been of assistance in my life. I have also called upon the other Archangels at times when help is needed with different life situations and I feel they have assisted me. So remember to talk to whichever Archangel you feel is appropriate for your issue and ask for their help. Then trust that they will assist you at the perfect time and in a way that is for your highest good. It's important to always thank the Archangels for their service.

Chapter 9

DERMATITIS

In the 1990's, a condition known as dermatitis started appearing on the fingers of my right hand. I was very interested to find out what caused it. Being very "new" at looking into the cause behind any ailment, seeking a Doctor's advice on how it could be treated was the best course of action to start with.

The first thing my Doctor said to me was that dermatitis wasn't curable as it would continue going through its' cycle only to do it all again and again indefinitely. She explained the cycle. It would just flare up, the prescribed cortisone ointment would need to be applied to dry up the blisters. Then it would be necessary to follow this up with a moisturiser on my hand and fingers because of the drying effect of the cortisone ointment.

Well the script she wrote for me was placed in my handbag. I wasn't sure at this stage if it would be filled, let alone use it because by now I believed that our reality is created by our thoughts. We have about 60,000 thoughts a day apparently and for every thought there is a feeling, and for every feeling there is a thought. That's a lot of thinking.

I further believe that I had the knowledge and power to heal my dermatitis, because I had created it through my thoughts and feelings. Once they were identified, the condition would be cleared and healed.

But on the other hand, I also know that others may not feel the same way and could be sceptical of my course of action. They would probably follow the Doctors' instructions without question because they know best.

From my understanding of metaphysics, thinking beyond the physical and into the mental and emotional realms, there had to be something, some thought pattern that was manifesting as dermatitis. The meaning for this condition is different when it is on the right hand compared to the left hand. There's a great analogy about an iceberg that is certainly relevant here. What you see on the top of the water is nothing compared to what is under the water line. This gave me an opportunity to look beneath the surface for the root cause and heal it from there.

So the books that I had on my shelf, and are used very often, *You Can Heal Your Life* by Louise L. Hay and *The Body is the Barometer of the Soul* by Annette Noontil, were consulted. What I read helped me understand what was happening, and discovered that dermatitis is - "Stirred up emotions of being unworthy or inadequate" and being my right hand is connected to my "physical being and doing". My feelings of inadequacy and unworthiness were constant companions throughout my life. Here was an opportunity to make some changes in my physical world.

It was time to make up a suitable affirmation to use to help correct my negative thinking/belief to a positive. (refer to Chapter 16, "Affirmations and How to Use Them"). The affirmation, "I love and accept myself exactly as I am now", was used as often as possible. Looking into a mirror and saying these words certainly added extra power to the exercise.

Now of course with some conditions, it's necessary to treat it topically as well. The next part of the exercise was checking in with my Angels to ask what, if anything, would help heal the dermatitis. You need to realise that being very naïve in this type of practice back then, trusting guidance received from the Angels didn't come easy. Guidance can come through a word, a feeling, a knowing or seeing a sign. In this case I heard the word "Thuja" which was unknown to me. Trusting the messages received this time was very important otherwise I'd always be looking outside myself for validation on everything.

The next stop was a natural health/organic store in Noosa and, guess what? Thuja was a legitimate herbal ointment. By applying the ointment as recommended, there was satisfying results almost straight away.

There's always something to be learnt from every condition. In this case, each time the dermatitis healed, the next time it would spread further up my hand. By continually affirming that it would stop before it got to my wrist, it did. Obviously the "root cause" of dermatitis had been identified and consequently healed as it has never returned. Another tick.

By the way – the script for the cortisone ointment was never filled.

Chapter 10

IN THE PRESENCE OF ANGELS

For a long time, asking the Angels to surround my car every time I went out anywhere was the normal thing to do. Believing in Angels, there was a certain knowing that they would be there, even if they weren't visible to me. Then one day, while asking my Angels to travel with me, they appeared, a vision of beautiful Angels all dressed in white, flying around my car like aeroplanes in formation. This made me laugh as it was so unexpected, but at the same time, it was very heart warming. Having proof sometimes is a wonderful thing. We're only human. So remember to ask the Angels to travel with you and you will be protected from harm. Belief is a powerful ally.

Angel story from York, England

Bill and I were on holiday in York, England, in 1996. We were walking along a street enjoying the serenity of our surrounds, when all of a sudden, church bells rang out. I was prompted to say at the time, "When the church bells ring, Angels get their wings." Looking up at that very moment, there in front of me was a building which displayed Angel statues on the parapet. The sign read "ANGEL HOUSE". What a wonderful sign and confirmation that the Angels were letting us know they were present. It's hard to describe the sheer delight I felt in that moment.

In 2001 after attending one of Doreen Virtue's seminars in Brisbane, my belief in Angels really intensified. On our way home we saw 444 on three different cars number plates and 444 means the Angels are all around. We felt very safe travelling back to Bundaberg even though it was late at night.

I take notice of numbers around me, believing they reveal significant and very meaningful messages for me.

In my experience, calling on the Angels for guidance and help in any situation has become natural for me to do. Over time, trust has been built between us, and their guidance is happily followed, if it feels right for me at that time.

My theory is, "If you believe, no proof is necessary; but if you don't believe, no proof is possible."

What do you believe?

Chapter 11

MY DATE WITH DESTINY

6th June, 1970 is a date that was going to change my life forever, but of course I didn't know that then.

My sister Janet and I were walking up Brunswick Street, Fortitude Valley in Brisbane on our way to work. She was going to Manchester Unity in the city, while I was on my way to the Coca-Cola factory in the Valley, to work in the office there.

A car pulled up with two guys in it. They said hello and offered us a ride, which we declined. The driver was known to us, and was "interested in Janet", but he had his friend Bill in the passenger seat who we didn't know. It turns out that we only lived two doors up from them in New Farm.

So the story goes that my sister and I go down to their place for a get together one night, music and a few drinks, and that was the start of the never ending story. Bill said it was "the legs in the mini skirt" that left the lasting impression on him.

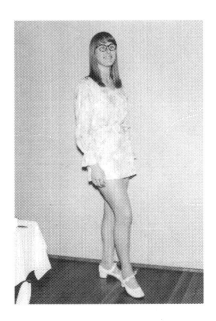

Bill and I continued dating for six months until he decided to go back to Port Moresby where there was the potential to make more money than in Brisbane. I had arranged to go to New Zealand with Janet and two friends we had met while working at the fruit cannery in Kyabram, Victoria, during the fruit picking season.

Well the ship to New Zealand was "dry docked". Bill suggested I come for a short visit to Port Moresby, all expenses paid, while waiting to go to New Zealand. How could I refuse an offer like that?

Off I went to Port Moresby for two weeks but then came back for my twenty-first birthday celebrations in April.

It wasn't too long before I decided to ditch the idea of going to New Zealand. Instead I packed up my belongings and went back to Port Moresby. Now Bill didn't know I was coming back. There were no mobile phones then, and he didn't have a normal phone. Posting a card with the news would've taken quite a while to get there. So apart from sending him a telegram which would've given him a fright, I just decided to go back. Obviously I trusted that everything would be all right.

He was a bit surprised to see me back but was quite happy and took it all in his stride. With the small flat that he rented, a car, and with my job at the Taxation Department, we were set.

Then the day came when I told him to hold out his hand, and as he did, I shook it and said, "Congratulations, you are going to be a daddy". Silence.

We got married in Port Moresby on 2nd July 1971 and by now you will realise that Leanne, our first child, was on the way and wanting to join us, and did so in early 1972.

Fast forward to 2001 when Bill and I separated.

It seemed to me that after thirty years together, our marriage had run its' course as I felt that Bill was never emotionally available for me. That was important. Whenever there were issues to discuss, he always had work to do at the office and would leave. Nothing ever seemed to get resolved. Frustration and resentment were a constant, which turned into anger and a lack of love for him and what we had.

In hindsight, this was a common pattern of the men in my life. That is why I kept attracting it to give me the opportunity to heal it. Unfortunately, I didn't know that at the time, so I chose to leave the relationship to save my sanity. It seemed futile to stay and work it all out. I needed time to reflect and understand what was happening.

After selling our home in Bundaberg, Bill moved to Brisbane and I relocated to Moore Park near Bundaberg with two friends.

Then a few months later I moved to Marcoola on the Sunshine Coast. We lived our separate lives until about July 2002 when Bill made contact and wanted to talk. As we had been apart for over a year, our plan was to discuss divorce, if we couldn't work things out. Was that what either of us wanted? So that day we met and talked, and talked. The most we had talked in years but still nothing had been resolved.

On my way back from that meeting I was driving along the coast road to Coolum when all of a sudden my head just turned to the right. There were these numbers, 1728, on the side of a building. Why was I being shown this? OMG as they say, they were Bill's (17) and my (28) birth dates. I just knew in that moment that we were meant to be together and that God had a bigger plan for our life. There was more to do and I knew divorce wasn't part of the plan. So now what?

We decided to give it another go and renewed our vows on 5.10.2002. These numbers add up to 10, which becomes a 1, meaning "New Beginnings" so it was all meant to be. I won't say it's been easy, (Bill will agree with that I'm sure), but it's all been worth it.

So, my date with destiny was set up in my pre-life choices. I now truly believe that my legs were the catalyst for us meeting. He just knew that I was "the one" he was meant to share his life with.

Here we are in 2018 still going strong, enjoying life, and travelling to wonderful places that we never had the opportunity to explore when we were young. We decided to have our family first. I have to admit we still have our challenges, and differences of opinions, but we are older and wiser now. We have both learnt a lot about ourselves as individuals, and each other as a couple. Now we have the tools through our life experiences and growth to hopefully deal with, and resolve, anything that comes along in a more positive way. Life is sweet!

Chapter 12

CANCER ... OR IS IT?
What I learnt from having a multi-coloured wart-like cancerous lesion on my vagina

It was 2001, and after having the appropriate pap smear and biopsy, I was given the diagnosis of Stage three vaginal cancer. My Doctor in Bundaberg advised me to have surgery as soon as it could be arranged because my life was in grave danger. I wasn't sure that this was the best course of action for me.

I learnt that:-

> It was important to pray about my diagnosis first and ask for the help I was going to need to heal the dis-ease that I believe I had created in my body. By surrendering the whole situation through prayer, it was fascinating to watch where the assistance came from. I trusted and followed the information given.

I learnt that:-

> The help and support of my like-minded friends were very important to me and of great

assistance in unravelling the mystery behind the formation of the lesion. I felt that my family may not be happy with my choices and the course of action I wanted to take. I chose not to tell any of my family, including my husband. All my energies were needed to focus on what needed to be done.

Although I didn't feel fearful about what was happening, I sensed my family would be. I found out about the cancer after Bill and I had separated. I felt that if he was meant to know, I would've known about my condition before that. All our children had moved away from Bundaberg and had happy, busy lives.

I learnt that:-

The renewed courage, trust, and belief in myself was necessary to navigate this unknown territory. I was also very grateful for the unconditional love and guidance from God, Jesus, the Angels of Love and Light, my spirit guides and teachers, and some very close friends.

I learnt that:-

Having an A1 physical body by taking all the prescribed vitamins and minerals, and following a holistic Doctor's dietary requirements for about four months, didn't make any difference to my condition. My lesion actually grew by fifteen percent and continued further up inside of me.

In that moment I knew I hadn't found the root cause of my cancer and that's when I got excited.

It's one of those light bulb moments that gets talked about a lot, I finally had clarity. On the way back to Bundaberg from my Doctor's visit in Brisbane, I was thinking about all that I could do to bring about the healing that was necessary. Surgery and drugs weren't included.

I learnt that:-

Once the core wound had been identified, which was being sexually molested when I was five years old, by someone who was well known to our family, I was able to set in motion the next stage of healing.

During this time, I had a dream where I was shown that my bottom was new and pink, just like a baby's bottom. I instantly knew that the cancer had been healed on the spiritual level. I just needed to do more healing work on the mental, emotional and physical levels. Feeling reassured, the journey continued.

Using the information in Louise L. Hay's book *You Can Heal Your Life*, the probable causes of cancer are:- "Deep hurt. Longstanding resentment. Deep secret or grief eating away at the self. Carrying hatreds. What's the use." I could relate to all of these.

The affirmations used were:- "I love and approve of myself. I choose to fill my world with joy." I set about using these straight away.

Forgiveness also played a huge role in freeing myself from the pain of the past. The affirmation recommended here was, "I forgive everyone, I forgive myself, I forgive all past experiences, and I am free." This was used for everyone that I had any unhealthy sexual association with, including the person who molested me.

Within a week of commencing this next level of understanding and healing, the lesion had dissolved completely. The root cause had been revealed and released/healed. It has been seventeen years since that happened.

It's interesting to note when the Doctor in Brisbane examined me and noticed that the lesion had gone, he asked me if I had put anything on it to make it go away. Of course I said, "No, it was healed from the inside". He certainly looked baffled but didn't ask any more questions.

I learnt that:-

Painful and traumatic memories can be locked away for a long time, in my case nearly fifty years, until we are ready and able to deal with them. The timing has to be right.

It explained:-

Why I only wanted daughters.

Why I was an overprotective mother and didn't like my girls sleeping over at other people's homes.

Why I felt I couldn't say no to anyone and accepted blame for everything. It must be my fault.

Why I've never felt safe and couldn't trust myself and others.

Why I kept attracting the wrong type of men and experiences into my life.

(My concept of what love would be like was very confused because of the environment I grew up in. My self-esteem was very low, so I wasn't very choosy with the men I dated and thought that it was acceptable to be treated badly.)

I now know:-

It was shocking to find out that I had been sexually molested when I was five. Although it wasn't my fault, it did change who I was and how I lived my life. This was obvious, particularly in the area of intimacy in relationships, and the somewhat misguided choices that were made.

I now know:-

That I needed time on my own to process the past experiences of my life. To take a good look at the reasons/root cause of why things happened the way they did. And to give me a greater understanding of who I really am.

I now know:-

That it was my opportunity to start loving myself so that I could be able to love others unconditionally as well. This has been an ongoing work-in-progress and will continue until I stop judging myself, and in turn, stop judging others and accept them for who they are.

I now know:-

> That there was a particular male in my life that always held me too close and too long, grabbing my bottom and so on. This made me feel very uncomfortable. One day, recently (2017), I realised that there was still some energy around me that he thought it was OK to do this type of thing and once I cleared that, he has stopped doing it. What a relief.

I now know:-

> That my parents (both deceased) now believe what happened to me. They came through giving their acknowledgement and support while I was having a healing with Caroline Rose, Heart Angel Healing Towards Souls Purpose. Caroline is able to connect with deceased loved ones and share messages that come through. It was an emotional time having their acknowledgement. I knew they hadn't believed me when I told them in 2001 after the lesion was healed.

I now know:-

> That I had been given a great opportunity to practice what I had been preaching in my workshops and study courses. From everything I had learned so far, it proved to me that it was all relevant and necessary for my positive outcome. It's something that I feel confident about to share with others now, and I had validated the saying, "Healer, heal thyself", which felt amazing!

While living at Marcoola in 2002 on the Sunshine Coast, I attended a Breakfast Club Meeting at Coolum. Members were invited to share a story if they felt inclined. Now I had no intention of speaking as listening to others is usually more insightful and entertaining than anything I could share.

The man sitting next to me could sense my need to speak and encouraged me to do so. Reluctantly I did. Briefly my cancer story was shared, and the outcome, lesion totally dissolved. A very proud moment for me.

But nothing prepared me for what came out of my mouth next, "I always wanted my Dad to be proud of me, maybe he was and maybe he wasn't, I don't know."

But in that moment by acknowledging how proud I was of myself and what I had achieved, there wasn't the same need to have it from my Dad any more. It felt so good and empowering. By cultivating qualities within myself, I will attract that from others.

Chapter 13

"ORBS" IN ISRAEL

While in Israel in 2013, I had the opportunity of touring the Old City of Jerusalem and visited some of the sacred sites. We were touring the Church of the Holy Sepulchre and the local guide pointed out to us that we were viewing Jesus' tomb, and the Ascension Chamber. Many photos were taken, but the awareness that orbs had shown up in some of them, wasn't evident until they were viewed after returning home.

With this realisation, the photos were submitted to The Diana Cooper Orb Team for an interpretation. Fortunately, they replied to my email (following) explaining what the orbs meant. It was so interesting as this amazing phenomenon had never shown up in my photos before. The orbs may appear to be attached to the walls, but based on the information I have read, orbs are actually energy floating in the atmosphere. Some may say that it could be rain drops, or condensation on the lens of the camera, but these photos were taken inside the building.

You can check out more information about Orbs on her website www.dianacooper.com and in her book *Ascension through Orbs* where Diana explains how orbs are now showing up in photos:-

Quote: "*Taking photographs of Orbs.* Orbs respond to the consciousness of the photographer. If your heart is open and you resonate at a fifth dimensional frequency, you can take orb photographs. Orbs are everywhere, day and night, but are more easily filmed at night in the rain! Having so said, we have both taken many beautiful orbs in the day. Why not use a digital camera, open your heart, call in the Angels, start clicking and see what happens?" End Quote. Good luck.

This is the email from The Diana Cooper Orb Team:-

Dear Lucy,

Thank you for your email.

Image – outside Jesus' tomb: There is energy present from Archangel Gabriel (purity), Archangel Michael (protection) and Mother Mary.

Image – Ascension Chamber: The energy is so high that it is attracting Angels, as well as other spiritual energy that is being helped with ascension. The people who are walking through this building are being blessed by the angelic energy.

Kind regards and Namaste
The Diana Cooper Orb Team
Janet Lawson

So from my understanding, I believe my energy was resonating at a fifth dimensional frequency at the time of taking the photos. This was all very new to me and I was totally fascinated by the whole experience.

From what I've read, the following is a short overview of the third, fourth and then living in a fifth dimensional reality, but still moving in and out of the other dimensions at times. How our soul evolves through learning and growing, which in turn clears and elevates our energy from fear to love.

Third Dimensional Reality - The Physical Realm

We live very much in the physical world where we feel we have to compete with everyone for our "slice of the pie" so to speak. Things such as money, material possessions, and relationships are very important to our happiness. We tend to be very judgemental and critical of others' lifestyles and points of view. Our life is characterised by polar opposites, right and wrong, good and bad, light and dark etc. and there is a need to identify ourselves with titles like parent, wife, son, job, salary and home owner, to validate who we are as a person.

Fourth Dimensional Reality - Consciousness Begins to Awaken

Here judgement still exists however with more spiritual themes. You may now describe yourself as awake, while others may still appear asleep. The attention has shifted from pursuits in the material world to the pursuit of knowledge and understanding which seem to be the key to fulfilment and happiness. You may take on a spiritually themed ego structure. In this case, you may judge those who still eat meat, watch the news or drive cars etc. Ego is the ultimate enemy and therefore your goal is to get rid of it.

Fifth Dimensional Reality - Unity Consciousness

The All is the One, and the One is the All, as consciousness begins to awaken even further, the ego drops and judgement begins to fade away. You realize that the darkness of the world is a direct reflection of the shadow that still exists inside you and you no longer try to change the world, but rather begin to heal yourself. The love that grows within begins to translate into compassion and understanding for the external world. Love is the weapon that truly holds power. You are no longer attached to labels but see yourself as ever changing consciousness. You have the power to create your perception of reality, nothing is inherently good or bad, and nothing has power over you or your reality unless you have agreed to it on some level. Judgement has now become discretion and you use it wisely. There is an understanding that God, The Universe, or Source, lies within you.

More information on this and other related subjects may be found on www.secretenergy.com.

Chapter 14

THE RESTORATION OF MY
NATURAL HEARING

I was always a tomboy. At a very early age I fell (or tried to fly) off our verandah of a high blocked Queenslander home. My Mum thought she'd find me unconscious or with a broken limb. But no, I picked myself up and walked up the steps to meet her. She was very relieved.

On our farm at about four years old, I was in the back of the blitz truck. It was loaded up with timber cases full of beans that had been picked and packed that day. I was having a wonderful time sitting on one of the cases and sliding up and down as the truck went up and down the hills. Next thing I know, the bean case with me on it slid off the back of the truck. Somehow I missed being hurt. My Dad certainly got a fright. He put me in the front of the truck for the rest of the ride home.

Around five, I climbed onto our tank stand only to fall off and sustained a nasty gash under my nose. This required a very quick trip to the hospital. Falling out of trees happened quite often and sleep walking was a regular night time activity even into my forties.

My husband Bill and I had our ups and downs with our business. Financial difficulties were created when we built our own premises (our dream). By the mid 1980's we had created a troublesome financial crisis by our ill-informed choices, and with interest rates climbing to twenty-three percent.

At this time I developed tinnitus in both ears. This consisted of squealing and noises (like my head was full of cicadas) all the time, which were hard to ignore. These noises were multiplied when I got emotional as well. After struggling with a lack of hearing for quite some time, it became very stressful to interact with other people. The screaming in my ears would get louder. The concentration of trying to understand what was being said, and responding with a suitable reply, was exhausting. So the day came, reluctantly, to seek help, and I had two hearing aids fitted. Wearing glasses became normal for me over the years, but I have to say I felt ashamed of my hearing aids and couldn't bear for people to see them. They did give me a better quality of life though and I wasn't so tired anymore.

In the mid 1990's I made the choice to start looking into why my hearing had diminished. My hearing was normal at birth, as far as I know. I sought out different healing modalities to help me with this. I believe that all the falls I had as a child contributed to the physical/nerve damage. There was also the emotional deafness as well created by my traumatic environment above, as well as the circumstances reported in Chapters 1 and 2 and beyond.

There is something I've realized over time, and that is, whatever happens in a family environment transfers energetically to the unborn child. Whether it be love, beautiful music, hunger, trauma, disharmony, every emotion is felt. This is what they expect to experience once they are in life because that is what they know. But of course, it is still all perfect because that is what the soul chooses before it incarnates. Unfortunately, this knowledge is cleverly wiped out of our consciousness once we are born. Then we have to re-remember, and learn, and heal. Hopefully we are able to accept it all and move forward with our soul's growth. When it's the right time of course. Once I realized all this, I started healing the issues behind my deafness because compromising my precious hearing was too high a price to pay.

The probable causes of tinnitus are:-

"Intolerant to the point of screaming. Refusal to listen. Not hearing the inner voice." Well this sounded like my truth and the build-up of circumstances had reached screaming point. So, in hindsight, I just don't think I wanted to hear any of it anymore. The affirmations used here were:- "I trust my Higher Self. I listen with love to my inner voice. I release all that is unlike the action of love." Forgiveness was an important practice as well.

After many years of doing this, I felt that all avenues had been explored. As my tinnitus had been healed, all therapy was stopped. My hearing aids were providing me with reasonable hearing so I was grateful for that and decided to get on with my life.

Then in September 2014, while visiting my good friend Linda Christa~Clay, my hearing was so poor that my quest began anew. This pushed me to do everything in my power to find the answers to my hearing loss. If I've been able to heal other issues through therapy, affirmations, and so forth, I felt that there was no reason why this couldn't be done to restore my natural hearing as well. So I did what I always do, praying for the help that was needed to uncreate/heal this condition. Using the intuitive prompts I was receiving through guidance, I set about looking for suitable therapists who could assist with this.

While at a Body Mind Spirit Festival in Brisbane in 2015, Caroline Rose, Heart Angel Healing Towards Soul Purpose, had a stall and was extolling the virtues of *Rahanni Celestial Healing*. Caroline and I seemed to click and we set up some time for Rahanni healing sessions. After a few healings, it was decided that it would be beneficial for me to become attuned to Practitioner Level One of this healing modality. I would have access to this beautiful energy as well to be used at any time.

The following information is quoted by Carol Anne Stacey, Founder of *Rahanni Celestial Healing*.

♥ Carol Stacey has been presented with the gift of Rahanni to help humanity at this critical time in our existence.
♥ What is Rahanni?
   It means 'Of one heart'.
♥ It vibrates on a pink ray of light, balancing the heart centre bringing forth love and compassion to each individual soul.
♥ Although it is thousands of years old, it is a new healing for the Age of Aquarius. Bringing truth, love, and compassion, changing the consciousness and opening the hearts of every man, woman and child.
   This will bring inner peace to the mind and healing to the physical body.
♥ There is no separation, we are from one divine energy source.
♥ Rahanni balances the masculine and feminine aspects of every man, woman and child.
♥ It releases our fears and any negative energy that we accumulate from our experiences on this earth.
♥ It will help us with communication and to gain control over our lives.
♥ The vibration of earth had to be raised for the energy to be sustained, this has now happened, moving from the third to the fourth dimension of reality.

- ♥ Rahanni is not based on one religion, it is our natural essence. Bringing balance to our mind and body … End of Quote.

Some of the Affirmations used for the intention of restoring my natural hearing:-

I am now open and receptive to hearing positive and wonderful comments about me and who I am.

I am grateful for my ability to hear well. And so it is.

I am ready to hear.

I am willing to hear.

I hear clearly now.

I hear clearly now without my hearing aids.

I am enjoying my natural hearing.

I am now enjoying my fully restored natural hearing.

My ears hear clearly and for that I am very grateful.

I am now receiving all the help I need to revitalize my natural hearing senses and to restore my hearing.

Rahanni and other specialized forms of healing conducted by Caroline Rose, Heart Angel Healing Towards Soul Purpose, have been used for about two years now and great progress has been made. Particularly in finding, identifying, and releasing traumas, and any other emotional and mental issues that contributed to my hearing loss.

Taking full responsibility for any healing is important though. I always follow my inner knowing for the timing of healings. I like to feel/know that everything from a previous healing has been processed before proceeding with the next healing. This approach has been applied to any healing work I've undertaken over many years.

But obviously there is still more to do. As of now, I still need to wear my two hearing aids, but continue to work on the restoration of my natural hearing. I believe that whatever happens will be for my highest good and will be in its' perfect and divine timing. Who knows, better hearing could come naturally, or in the form of some new technology. Amazing things are happening all the time. So for now "I lovingly accept that everything is as it's meant to be." Amen.

Chapter 15

EXERCISE

Exercise has never been one of my favourite pastimes whereas some people just love it. Getting hot and sweaty makes me feel undignified, and especially with a face as red as a beetroot.

Now, I've done the walking, pedalled an exercise bike on the back deck looking out over my beautiful nature reserve while saying my affirmations. And I could even do this when it was raining, so there were no excuses. Sounds perfect doesn't it. Yoga classes entertained me for a while, even joined Pilates once but none of them lasted very long. I was always reasonably enthusiastic about it all to start with, because that does help. But there seemed to be an excuse, sometimes lame and sometimes not so lame, lurking in the back of my mind. Even a phone call seemed more important than doing some exercise and I could legitimately play hooky then. So it didn't take long, each time, to pack away the yoga mat, exercise gear, and the running shoes. Out of sight, out of mind, and I could then get on with my day pursuing more pleasurable activities.

Over the years, the same thoughts had been going around and around in my head. It must be time to get serious about my lifestyle and make some long overdue changes. There's no need to try certain clothes on to see if they still fit because I already knew they didn't. Well, I was going to be sixty-seven soon, and who knows I could live to be a hundred, so it was time!

The day of reckoning came. While at our local shopping centre, there it was, in the middle of the aisle, right in my path, a stand extolling the benefits of Curves. A 30 minute circuit training programme designed specifically for women. And it was in air-conditioned premises. Maybe it was time for me to re-evaluate my thoughts on exercise. The fact that the colour theme was purple, and purple being my favourite colour, I felt it was a positive sign. I was offered a weeks' free trial to see how I felt about it. After the trial, I decided to sign up for a year, yes, a whole year! Well it was cheaper to do it that way. As they say, nothing ventured, nothing gained.

Using the affirmation "I love and approve of myself exactly as I am" while doing the circuit definitely keeps me in a positive state of mind. No matter what the results are at the end, I still love and approve of myself. So I'm happy because I know I've done the best I could.

Well here we are in 2018, and this is my second year at Curves. While I haven't achieved the results that I thought I would or could, some noticeable progress has been made. I've lost a few kilos, my sleeping patterns have improved, and I have better flexibility. Obviously exercise has its' benefits as the advertisements keep saying, so it's onwards and upwards from here. Better results, better health, better body! Stay tuned for the next exciting episode.

Chapter 16

AFFIRMATIONS AND HOW TO USE THEM

Affirmations were first made known to me after reading Louise L. Hay's book *You Can Heal Your Life* over 30 years ago. In her book, Louise talks about the "Probable Cause" behind any ailment, and a "New Positive Thought Pattern" to help correct whatever is out of balance in your body, mind and emotions. Affirmations are always said in a positive way and that whatever you are striving for is already here.

Before I started writing this book I made up an affirmation to use which was:

"I am totally capable of writing a collection of memoirs for my book *For the Love of Self* and any information that needs to be included will be revealed to me at the right time." And so it is!

Be aware though that your subconscious mind doesn't understand negatives.

Changing negatives to positives:

"I don't want to be like my Mum or Dad" can be changed to "I am my own person."

When someone asks you how you are, do you say, "Oh not bad" (double negative) so it would be better to say, "I'm really good thanks."

"I don't get sick" is very different from "I am well and happy all the time". The first affirmation is focusing on sick even though you say you "don't" want to be, whereas the second affirmation is saying well and happy, and the mind accepts that. Can you see the difference?

*I would like to relay a story here to help you better understand what I'm saying.

The story goes that my husband, but only seventeen at the time, wanted to buy his first car. Now he knew he didn't want a blue Falcon station wagon with automatic gears. But guess what he bought, exactly that. This happened because he didn't really know what he wanted and he manifested what he kept thinking about. Fascinating.*

So many times in life we seem to get what we don't want only because we don't know what we do want.

As Louise quotes, "Your thoughts and beliefs of the past have created this moment, and all the moments up to this moment. What you are now choosing to believe and think and say will create the next moment and so on." Therefore, it's important to be mindful of your thoughts, approximately about 60,000 a day, so negative thoughts can be changed to positives as they happen, if you catch them that is.

You can always use the affirmations that Louise has written in her book, or you can make up your own, or use a combination of both like I do. This can help change a condition, illness, disease, or unhealthy situation.

Some examples:

"I love and accept myself exactly as I am now" is a great start to making changes because when we can love ourselves, perceived imperfections and all, we can begin to change some of the limiting thoughts and beliefs that aren't working for us.

"My nutritious eating habits are reflected in my clear mind and healthy body." This could help you change some of your unhealthy eating habits.

"I lovingly and willingly release the need for ... (substance). eg Nicotine. (This certainly helped me finally give the cigarettes away after thirty years.)

"I forgive everyone, I forgive myself, I forgive all past experiences and I am free" is a very powerful affirmation to use. I believe everyone has someone to forgive, even themselves, for wrong doings, whether intentional or not. I have found forgiveness to be one of the most important, and life changing, exercises that I have used.

Also I like to use affirmations starting with I AM eg. "I AM kind", "I AM loving and lovable", "I AM a compassionate person". "I AM on Spirit Time" which means you always have enough time for anything even if you don't think you have. And so on.

Another favourite of mine is, "I live and let live, I let go and I let God". It certainly helps to surrender any situation and wait for the solution to be revealed. Eventually you'll know what to do. It also helps to not judge someone or their life, and wanting to change it for the better, or so we think. No one ever knows someone else's full story.

If you are feeling fearful for any reason, you may find it helpful to use "Never fear, Christ and the Angels are near". It certainly helps me when I'm feeling overwhelmed.

Using positive affirmations everyday keeps me in a calmer state of mind, and therefore, creating positive outcomes. This is where gratitude comes in. Writing at least five, or more, things that you are grateful for in a journal every day certainly increases the flow of good that comes into your life.

So you can start today:-

I am grateful for this beautiful sunny day.

I am grateful for my family, friends, job.

I am grateful for our electricity and technology.

I am grateful for our clean hot and cold running water.

There is no limit to being grateful. Just watch the magic happen!

The Serenity Prayer is also very useful for any situation that I feel I want to control or change that may not be in my best interest. So reciting this prayer/affirmation a few times helps me feel more balanced and peaceful about everything. If there is some course of action to take, it is done with clarity and love.

CONCLUSION

My book is about giving people hope. It's been said, "Where there's life, there's hope." It's also true that "Where's there's hope, there's life." Hope is the confidence – the positive expectations – that something good is going to happen. Hope enhances life!

The strategies and tools in this book can be aligned to any ailment that you have. It's going beneath the surface to find out what's going on. This gives us the clues to healing any imbalance or dis-ease in our mind and body. You may find that some of the causes have been disguised/hidden for most of our lives.

Many lessons have been learnt so far, and much healing has taken place through the use of alternative/complementary therapies. Great comfort, and intuitive guidance, have also been received from God, Jesus, the Angels of Love and Light, and my spirit guides and teachers. I believe they are always near and offering their love and support in any way that is for my highest good at any moment.

Faith and trust in a higher power greater than myself, call it what you like – God, Universe, The Divine, Infinite Power, have helped me know and believe that anything is possible.

Be not afraid to reach out to this higher power, no matter what your religious or spiritual beliefs may be. I just know that you won't ever feel alone again. You will know that there is always someone to talk to who will listen, uninterrupted, with non-judgement and unconditional love.

ACKNOWLEDGEMENTS

I wish to acknowledge the following people for their devotion to my spiritual development and healing successes which have been instrumental in the writing of this book.

Linda Christa~Clay, good friend, Messenger of the Angels & Spiritual Clairvoyant Healer, who always has her heart and ears open for all that I need to share.

Faye Wenke who taught me the importance of having Reiki in my life and attuned me through First Degree, Second Degree, and onto Masters Level in Reiki *Jin Kei Do.*

Leonie Bartlett, Reiki *Jin Kei Do* Master, good friend and Freelance Graphic Designer who is responsible for the cover art work of this book.

Janine from Crystal Love who helped me trust my intuition.

Caroline Rose, Heart Angel Healing Towards Soul Purpose, for attuning me to *Rahanni Celestial Healing* and conducting many other in-depth healing sessions to release my traumas with her loving attention.

Yvonne Webb, author of *The Scholar Explorer,* for her patience in "How to Write a Biography" class, and invaluable guidance.

The many teachers and healers who have crossed my path and shared their healing, and wisdom, for which I'm very grateful.

My husband Bill for his love and support throughout, and for never giving up on me or us.

TITLES OF RELATED INTEREST

You Can Heal Your Life
The Power is Within You
By: Louise L. Hay
www.hayhouse.com

The Body is the Barometer of the Soul
By: Annette Noontil

Healing with the Angels
Angel Numbers
By: Doreen Virtue PhD
www.AngelTherapy.com

Love is in the Earth
(A Kaleidoscope of Crystals)
By: Melody

A Return to Love
By: Marianne Williamson
www.marianne.com

Journey of Souls
Destiny of Souls
By: Michael Newton PhD
www.newtoninstitute.org
www.llewellyn.com

Ascension through Orbs
Light up your Life
By: Diana Cooper
www.dianacooper.com

Linda Christa~Clay
Messenger of the Angels & Spiritual Clairvoyant Healer
Mobile: 0403 514 177

Faye Wenke
Reiki Jin Kei Do Master
www.reikijinkeido.com.au

Leonie Bartlett
Reiki Jin Kei Do Master
Freelance Graphic Designer
www.facebook.com/ellaginspired

Caroline Rose
Heart Angel Healing Towards Soul Purpose
www.heartangel.com.au

Go to www.KayleneHay.com.au to order
your copy of For the Love of Self.
Or Contact Kaylene at lucylight11@bigpond.com

Notes

Notes

Printed in the United States
By Bookmasters